INTERNATIONAL

English Foundation

Activity Book A

T0337531

Published by Collins
An imprint of HarperCollins*Publishers*
The News Building, 1 London Bridge Street,
London, SE1 9GF, UK

HarperCollins Publishers

Macken House, 39/40 Mayor Street Upper,
Dublin 1, D01 C9W8, Ireland

Browse the complete Collins catalogue at
www.collins.co.uk

10 9 8 7 6 5 4

ISBN 978-0-00-846856-9

British Library Cataloguing-in-Publication Data
A catalogue record for this publication is available from the British Library.

Author: Fiona Macgregor
Publisher: Elaine Higgleton
Product manager: Letitia Luff
Commissioning editor: Rachel Houghton
Edited by: Hannah Hirst-Dunton
Editorial management: Oriel Square
Cover designer: Kevin Robbins
Cover illustrations: Jouve India Pvt Ltd.
Internal illustrations: Jouve India Pvt. Ltd.,
p 2, 4, 6 Sahitya Rani, p 8–9 Sylwia Filipczak,
p 15–18 Tomislav Zlatic
Typesetter: Jouve India Pvt. Ltd.
Production controller: Lyndsey Rogers

Printed in India by Multivista Global Pvt. Ltd.

Acknowledgements

With thanks to all the kindergarten staff and their schools around the world who have helped with the development of this course, by sharing insights and commenting on and testing sample materials:

Calcutta International School: Sharmila Majumdar, Mrs Pratima Nayar, Preeti Roychoudhury, Tinku Yadav, Lakshmi Khanna, Mousumi Guha, Radhika Dhanuka, Archana Tiwari, Urmita Das; Gateway College (Sri Lanka): Kousala Benedict; Hawar International School: Kareen Barakat, Shahla Mohammed, Jennah Hussain; Manthan International School: Shalini Reddy; Monterey Pre-Primary: Adina Oram; Prometheus School: Aneesha Sahni, Deepa Nanda; Pragyanam School: Monika Sachdev; Rosary Sisters High School: Samar Sabat, Sireen Freij, Hiba Mousa; Solitaire Global School: Devi Nimmagadda; United Charter Schools (UCS): Tabassum Murtaza and staff; Vietnam Australia International School: Holly Simpson

The publishers wish to thank the following for permission to reproduce photographs.

(t = top, c = centre, b = bottom, r = right, l = left)

p 20 kazoka/Shutterstock, p 20 bluedog studio/Shutterstock,
p 20 Romolo Tavani/Shutterstock, p 20 Fotokostic/Shutterstock

MIX
Paper | Supporting
responsible forestry
FSC™ C007454

This book contains FSC™ certified paper and other controlled sources to ensure responsible forest management.

For more information visit: www.harpercollins.co.uk/green

Trace

Trace over the dotted lines.
Finish the picture.

Date:

Draw

Draw your face on the easel.

Date:

Match

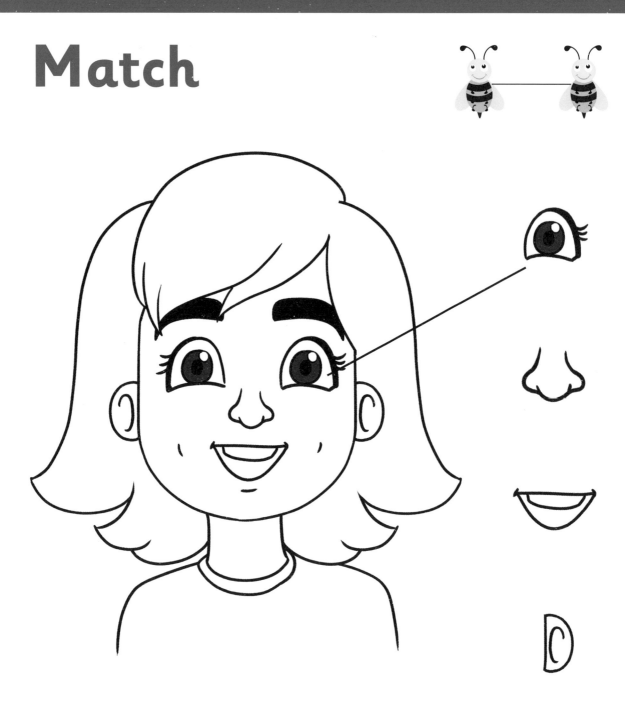

Draw lines to match the parts to the main picture.

Date:

Follow

 -------

 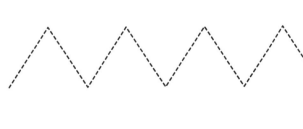 

Follow the dots to draw lines from the backs to the fronts of the children.   Date:

Trace and say

S S S S S

S S S S

Sam

Trace the letters. Say the sound.
Try writing some more.

Date:

Trace

I am

Trace the letters. Stick or draw a picture.
Your teacher will help you write your name.   Date:

Match

Gran

Mum

Jen

Dad

Match the people to what they do in the story.

Date:

Find

Dad

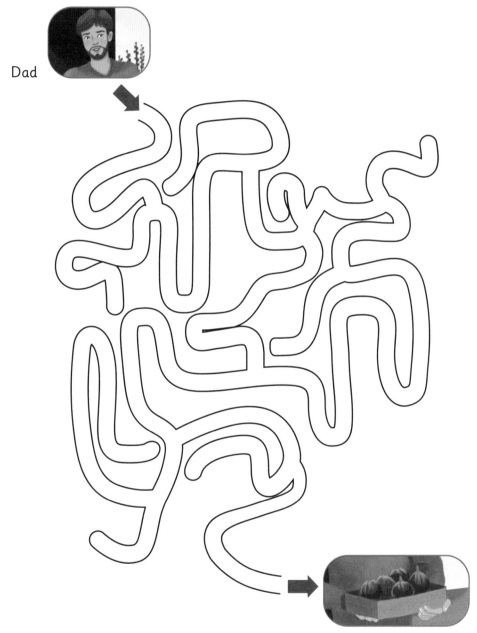

Figs

Draw a line and help Dad find the figs.

Date:

Trace and say

ant

Trace the letters. Say the sound.
Try writing some more.

Date:

Circle

Circle all the things that start with the 's' sound.
Colour them in.

Date:

Follow

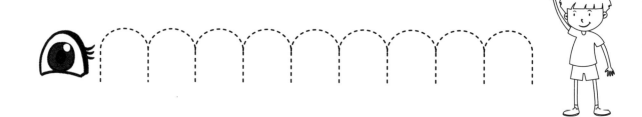

Follow the lines. Use different colours.

Date:

Draw

I see.

I smell.

Draw something you can see.
Draw something you like to smell.

Date:

Trace and say

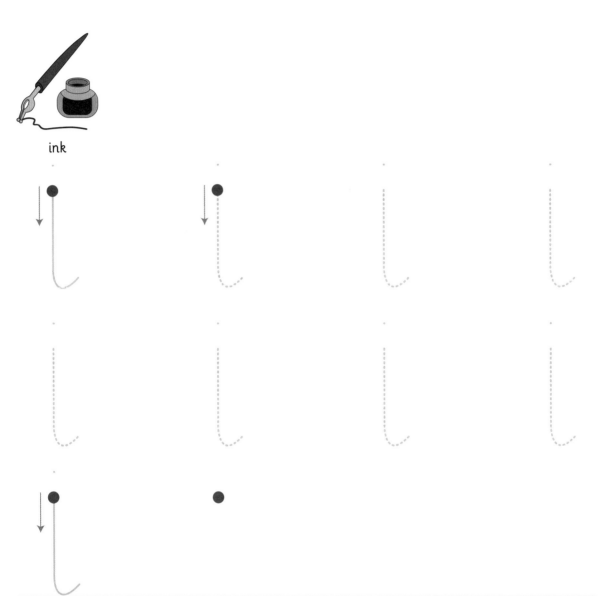

ink

Trace the letters. Say the sound.
Try writing some more.

Date:

Put in order

1 **2** **3** **4**

Number the pictures to match
the order of the story.

Date:

Find

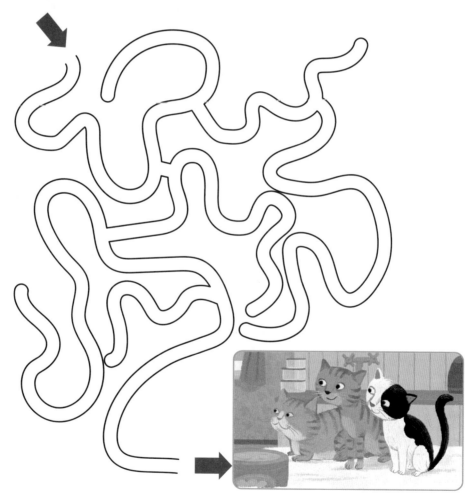

Draw a line and help Pam find the cats.   Date:

Trace and say

Pam

Trace the letters. Say the sound.
Try writing some more.

Date:

Trace and say

Tim

Trace the letters. Say the sound.
Try writing some more.

Date:

Follow

Follow the dots to draw a plant.
Colour in the plant.

Date:

Put in order

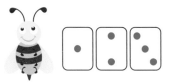

1 2 3 4

Number the pictures to show what you need
to grow a plant. Use the numbers 1 to 4.   Date:

Draw

Draw your own plant.

Date:

Alphabet time

ant

ball

cat

duck

Alongside structured phonics lessons, you may want to display and talk about one letter of the alphabet in an 'alphabet time' session each week.

Alphabet time

egg

fish

grapes

hat

Assessment record

_____ has achieved these English Foundation Phase Objectives:

Reading

R1 Become aware of sound structures in language	1	2	3
R2 Develop pre-reading skills	1	2	3
R3 Recognise some letters of the English alphabet	1	2	3
R4 Understand and explore the link between letters and the sounds they represent	1	2	3
Reading motor skills	1	2	3

Writing

W1 Develop pre-writing skills	1	2	3
Writing motor skills	1	2	3

Speaking

S1 Be able to express oneself in everyday situations	1	2	3
S2 Understand sentences	1	2	3
Speaking developmental skills	1	2	3

Listening

L1 Know how to listen and respond appropriately in everyday contexts	1	2	3
Listening developmental skills	1	2	3

1: Partially achieved
2: Achieved
3: Exceeded

Signed by teacher:
Signed by parent: Date: